Shakespeare And Democracy...

Edward Salmon

Crown 4to.   3s. 6d. Net

THE RUSSIAN GARLAND

Edited by

ROBERT STEELE

With Six Illustrations by

J. R. DE ROSCISZEWSKI

"The Russian Garland" is a translation of a number of folk-tales selected from a collection of popular chap-books brought together at Moscow in the early years of the nineteenth century. They are the chosen stories of the urban peasant, which have taken shape and survived by his favour, gathered from many lands, from India to Provence. The illustrations, drawn for this edition, are faithful expressions of the feelings of the story-teller, and add no little to the permanent value of the book.

"Perhaps the most distinguished child's book of the year."—*Evening Standard.*

McBRIDE, NAST & CO., LTD.

A

Crown 8vo.   5s. Net

THE FOOLS OF SHAKESPEARE

by

FREDERICK WARDE

It was Gratiano who said, "Let me play the fool," and to play one of the fools of Shakespeare has been the ambition of many great actors. There have been critics who have contended that Shakespeare got the essentials of all humanity in his jesters, and that the Fool in "King Lear" is the greatest part in the play. Mr. Warde in his comprehensive study makes the first attempt of the kind to be found in the vast volume of Shakespearean commentary. An actor himself, he interprets Shakespeare with as much skill between the boards as on the boards. It is an unconventional book.

McBRIDE, NAST & CO., LTD

SHAKESPEARE AND DEMOCRACY

By

EDWARD SALMON

Author of " The Life of James Wolfe," " The
Life of Admiral Sir Charles Saunders," " The
Story of the Empire," &c.

London   New York

1916

PRINTED BY THE WESTMINSTER PRESS,
411A HARROW ROAD, LONDON, W.

By Way of Introduction

SHAKESPEARE has been with us three hundred years ; in the world of intellect he is our priceless national possession. Democracy, as we know it in Great Britain, has been with us thirty years ; it is the most remarkable of all democracies because under a strictly constitutional régime, it is called upon to face the responsibilities of an Empire composed partly of other democracies and partly of dependencies. It is a democracy unlike that either of France or the United States of America. In this Tercentenary year of Shakespeare's death what is the message of his works for the Empire and for Democracy ? Shakespeare is regarded as the fount of wisdom in most things, politics apart : the party man has looked at him through party spectacles falsely focussed. It is humiliating evidence of the dwarfing effect of party on the national mind that with rare exceptions even Shakespeare has been victimized by its bias.

This essay is an attempt to show that Shakespeare as revealed in his works was as superior to any mere party or class feeling as it is possible for mortal to be. His patriotism, on which Sir Sidney Lee and others have discoursed so eloquently, and his detachment from the active forces of the spacious days in which he played and wrote, would in themselves supply a guarantee that he who could see, good in everything would not find ill alone in the meanest of his fellow creatures.

The view of Shakespeare and Democracy which I venture to set forth is not a recent discovery to meet the occasion either of the Tercentenary or the new spirit which the Prussian menace has brought into our national life. Some passages from this essay which have appeared in print, have been challenged by the Doubting Thomases of party as though a con-census of opinion among the critics necessarily implied Truth and the Last Word. Its substance once formed the subject of a lecture, followed by a discussion ; not a single speaker would admit that Shakespeare was other than a Tory devoid of sympathy with the common people. If my little effort, the result of years of study of all that has been said on Shakespeare as politician, does not show the folly of tearing text from context and the unfairness of fathering the views of *dramatis personæ* on the playwright, then we must despair of all comment-ary. As well might we make Shakespeare a murderer because he was the author of *Macbeth* or a lunatic because he wrote *King Lear*.

Dr. Stubbs was once asked what he thought of Shakespeare's "very evident feudal disdain of the democracy." He answered that Shakespeare was not a modern democrat : in the Tudor period the people, he said, had not yet emerged, but in his opinion " Shakespeare was too human and too permanent—shall we say eternal ?—to be a party politician. 'A plague on both your houses ' is his nearest to a political cry."

And that may be taken as the moral alike of this essay and of the crisis through which " this England " that Shakespeare loved so well, is passing to-day. Shakespeare had many messages for mankind, but none more valuable or more opportune than that party is a national bane. That message is implicit, if not explicit, in his works.

The Poet and the Essayist

SHAKESPEARE has in his time played many parts. To the Essayist he has been a century-long boon. He has been considered as historian, as artist, as dramatist, as moralist, as theologian, but except casually and in passing, not as politician, and particularly not as democrat. What is a democrat? I conceive a democrat to be one who admits all classes to political power. If we think of the times in which Shakespeare lived, when the monarch might claim divine right without appearing ridiculous, we shall not be surprised if we find Shakespeare taking the monarchical view, but if we further remember how much he owed to Plutarch neither will it be surprising if we find him Republican too.

In my judgment the only fair verdict on Shakespeare from the political point of view is that imbibing monarchism in the air he breathed, and republicanism in much that he read, he absorbed the best of both. So far as we can trace allusions to his political leanings in commentaries on his life and works it seems to have been the habit to regard him as a plain unvarnished Tory. It was indeed Hazlitt's view that the cause of the people was hardly a subject for poetry. " There is," said Hazlitt, " nothing heroical in a multitude of miserable rogues not wishing to be starved or complaining that they are likely to be so, but when a single man comes forward to brave their cries and to make them submit to the last indignities from mere pride or self will, our admiration of his prowess is immediately converted into contempt for their pusillanimity." Here we get some clue to the standpoint taken by the party student of Shakespeare. To Hartley Coleridge he was a Tory and a gentleman ; to Lord Morley a feudalist ; Professor Brandes speaks of his anti-democratic bias ; Professor Dowden had doubts whether he should label Shakespeare Liberal or Conservative ; to Mr. William Archer he was an aristocrat and a snob ; Mr. Frank Harris writes of his " aristocratic leanings," his detestation of the Commons, his contempt for mere citizens ; Mr. Charles Whibley links him with Aristophanes and " all the greatest of the Poets " as " a sound Tory " ; on the other hand to Swinburne he was something of a Socialist ; to Mr. L. T. Etty he was a true son of the Renaissance with natural literary sympathy with Republican aspirations. Shakespeare's aristocratic bias, says Mr. Harris, narrowed his vision of life.

More than one critic has pointed out that Shakespeare attributes all the glory of Agincourt to the King, and does not so much as mention an archer.

SHAKESPEARE AND DEMOCRACY

It is forgotten that Henry V makes a speech before Agincourt in which he describes himself and his followers as a band of brothers, assuring them that this day shall gentle the condition even of the most vile and that gentlemen in England will hold themselves accursed they were not with the army on St. Crispin's day. It *is* remarkable that in *King John* there is no allusion, however vague, to the Great Charter. The omission struck me forcibly long ago, and I find Professor Brandes refers to it at some length, attributing the fact to Shakespeare's discreet regard for the susceptibilities of Queen Elizabeth, who did not wish to be reminded of the rights of the people. If many passages in his plays did not attest otherwise, the omission might be taken as proof that Shakespeare was indifferent alike to what we call progress and to the common cause. There is ample material in his plays, as I shall hope to show, to enable us to understand the impressions which ate deep into his heart from his reading of history. To get the key to Shakespeare's own views on many things his work must be read as a whole and not regarded piecemeal. We shall at least be on surer ground than was the discoverer of the cypher which proved that Shakespeare was not himself but another—the greatest impersonation and alibi in all history. Isolated passages may, of course, represent anybody or nobody. They may be a faithful historic record, they may have been an expression of the writer's own sentiments or they may have been merely what he considered a particular person in a particular position would say.

When, however, individuals who bear no sort of resemblance to each other give publicity to the same sentiments, we may take it that we have hit upon the writer's estimate of things generally. Shakespeare has left this opportunity open for ascertaining what he thought on political matters to a degree which seems to me conclusive. Whether he did so by design or not is immaterial. The chances are that quite unconsciously he leavened diverse characters with a little leaven of his own great self whilst identifying himself with none in particular.

Is Shakespeare Self-Revealed ?

SIR SIDNEY LEE, to whose industrious search for biographic material we owe so much, has never regarded it as possible to rescue the tangible personality of the poet from his dramatic art. He once provoked an illuminating essay from Professor Edward Dowden entitled " Is Shakespeare Self-Revealed ? " Professor Dowden pointed out that a number of persons not given to the pursuit of will-o'-the-wisps, among them Masson, Ingram, Bagehot, Leslie Stephen, Goldwin Smith, Bradley, Raleigh have sought to discover the man Shakespeare in his works, and by various methods managed to paint portraits of Shakespeare which resemble each other at least as closely as portraits painted from a real face at various points of view by artists " indifferent honest." Sir Sidney Lee sought frequent pronouncements in Shakespeare's writings on religion, ethics, political economy, and the like, and found quite opposite statements on one and the same matter uttered by the several *dramatis personæ*. " Now," said Professor Dowden, " among the portrait painters there is a substantial agreement as to Shakespeare's opinions on some of the topics named by Dr. Lee , they represent him, if not as ' a Tory and a gentleman,' at least as leaning, like Scott and the mature Goethe, towards a conservative view in social and political affairs ; not as a revolutionary spirit, governed by doctrinaire abstractions, yet as one who sympathised with the trials and sorrows of the poor ; a man who disliked mobs, and distrusted the politics of the citizen class as self-interested and narrow ; one who perceived the value of what Ulysses terms ' degree.' They say that he was not a religious enthusiast nor a theological dogmatist ;

that he did not, like Shelley, set himself against existing beliefs ; that he was no Puritan ; that he had a spirit of reverence and a deep sense of the mystery of things." It was Professor Dowden's view—a view it is a little difficult to accept—that a man's opinions, though an important part of the contents of his mind, are often not a distinguishing part of his personality. More important than the opinions themselves is the way he holds them ; in other words, " le style, c'est l'homme "—surely with some modern instances in mind, a rather dangerous dictum. Professor Dowden continues : " That Shakespeare could see two sides of a question and could put opposite views of truth into the mouths of different persons is in itself a distinguishing feature of his mind. It is not every man who can do this, nor every poet. We learn that whatever conclusion Shakespeare arrives at on this subject or on that,

he will not hold it in a shrill, eager,
intolerant way; he can see things in
the round; he can understand another
man's point of view; he cannot be
what Professor William James styles
a ' thin ' thinker; his way of thinking
is essentially ' thick.' Now to learn
this is to learn much. Two men hold-
ing antagonistic opinions, if they hold
them in the same way, resemble each
other mentally much more than do
two men who hold identical opinions
in different ways. The heads of Poysam
the Puritan and Charbon the Papist
may be of one build. New presbyter
may be very like old priest if both are
shrill and intolerant, or like, again, if
both are the reverse of ' thin ' and
extravagant in their mode of belief.
If we are sure that Shakespeare could
see and feel every side of a question
we already know a very remarkable
characteristic of his intellect."

Dowden clearly did not share
Ruskin's view that Shakespeare was

not only unknowable but inconceivable. But then Ruskin, whilst admitting the power of Shakespeare over him, was inclined to wonder whence the power came or what was its worth. Shakespeare gave him the wrong Kings—a quaint conceit that—and spoilt the loveliest plays by the introduction of undesirable characters. It was Ruskin's misfortune to find the wisdom of Shakespeare so useless that " at this time of being and speaking among active and purposeful Englishmen I know no one who shows a trace of ever having felt a passion of Shakespeare's or learnt a lesson from him." Ruskin's knowledge of the " active and purposeful Englishman " we can only conclude was like Sam Weller's of London in one respect : it was peculiar.

The Brandes-Archer View

SOME years ago Sir Herbert Beer-bohm Tree addressed a Poplar audience on the subject of the Humanity of Shakespeare—a humanity that has never been denied even by those who do not agree that Shakespeare held any other than narrow Tory views. A young man in the audience asked whether Shakespeare did or did not ridicule the working classes, and Mr. Will Crooks, who was in the chair, disallowed the question, whilst Sir Herbert remained silent. Mr. William Archer took the question as the text for an essay, in which he suggested that Shakespeare had no sympathy with the working classes simply because he did not foresee the coming of democracy. " There is," said Mr. Archer, " no getting round the fact that Shakespeare was an aristocrat, and what we should nowadays call a bit of a snob. He had the exaggerated contempt of the parvenu for all who stood at, or below, his own original level. His gentility was not inborn, but acquired, and therefore aggressive. If the young man of Poplar should resort, as Mr. Crooks suggested, to the Free Library, and should there refer to the eleventh chapter of the third book of Brandes's *William Shakespeare*, he will find a most unsavoury selection of references, running through the poet's whole career, to the physical characteristics of the common people. The comment by the Danish critic runs thus : ' The number of these passages proves that it was, in plain language, their evil smell which repelled Shakespeare. . . The good qualities and virtues of the people do not exist for him ; he believes their sufferings to be either imaginary or induced by their own faults. Their struggles are ridiculous to him, and their rights a fiction ;

their true characteristics are accessibility to flattery and ingratitude toward their benefactors ; and their only real passion is an innate, deep, and concentrated hatred of their superiors ; but all these qualities are merged in this chief crime : they *stink*.' Now, no one who visits Shakespeare's birthplace in Henley Street, Stratford-on-Avon, and imagines it as it must have been, in the fifteen-seventies and eighties, can believe that the family of John Shakespeare, butcher, maltster, leather dealer, etc., were very stringent in their ablutions, or that the neighbours with whom they consorted were scrupulous in removing the honourable sweat whereby they gained their bread. The poet's sensitiveness in such matters though no doubt real enough, must have been acquired after he came to London, and was admitted to the society of men of a higher rank than his own. The indelicacy with which his delicacy is expressed is very significant. The man of innate breeding neither feels nor expresses such bitterness of contempt for the physical or mental shortcomings of those who have not his advantages. Therefore, I repeat, we cannot get away from the admission that Shakespeare was a snob, inasmuch as he adopted with ostentation the tastes and prejudices of a class superior to his own. That trumpery coat-of-arms is a damning symbol."

⁊⸱ Much nearer a true appreciation of Shakespeare's attitude to the working classes was Swinburne when he wrote of " the kindly and faithful satire—if satire indeed we may call it—levelled at the sturdy assurance and stolid rectitude of the typical English plebeian." Mr. Archer is, of course, a good Radical ; he always has been, and his art as dramatist and his judgment as dramatic critic have never risen superior to his political bias. He falls far short of Shakespeare in that respect. Nothing could well be more ridiculous, nor more hopelessly misapprehend the business of the dramatist than Mr. Archer's attempt to prove that a democratic state was " in Shakespeare's eyes literally preposterous—a polity in which

> . . . Gentry, title, wisdom
> Cannot conclude, but by the yea or no
> Of general ignorance."

There is no more ground for fixing that view upon Shakespeare than for linking up the lines with a reference to Ulysses in *Troilus and Cressida*, as Mr. Archer did. It was the angry utterance of Coriolanus, and let it be said that if Coriolanus had not held such views the play itself would have been impossible. Even though Shakespeare sympathised with Coriolanus' statement that would not make him hostile to democracy, unless democracy is to be accepted as " general ignorance." Mr. Archer, in company with Professor Brandes, endorses a mere travesty of Shakespeare on this particular issue. True, he makes an effort to get some sort of perspective into his picture, and he concedes that Shakespeare wrote in days when Democracy in its modern sense was as unknown as the Motor 'Bus and the Tube. But one would have imagined that Mr. Archer would have looked at Shakespeare whole, and been inclined to note with eager approval that the man who lived throughout the reign of Queen Elizabeth and during the first dozen years of James I, was capable of uttering sentiments which—the most advanced democrat might claim—support the entire democratic case.

Mr. Algernon Cecil, in his life of Robert, the first Earl of Salisbury, affords a hint why Shakespeare— Robert Cecil's contemporary—must necessarily have taken a cautious line in dealing with affairs, ancient or otherwise. " The tragedies of Shakespeare, revolving as they do around the subjects of treachery, are a lasting reminder of the part which treason and plot played in the life of the sixteenth century." Not an atmosphere to foster democratic views—yet such views, I think, we shall find were not beyond Shakespeare. And for the reason that his sympathies were all embracing in an age which witnessed the divine pretensions of Kings, the beginnings of Empire, and the first real stirrings of the people to secure a recognition of their rights. " It is truly a lordly spectacle how this great soul takes in all kinds of men and objects, a Falstaff, an Othello, a Juliet, a Coriolanus ; sets them all forth in their round completeness ; loving, just, the equal brother of all " —so wrote the author of *Past and Present*.

To attack Shakespeare as an aristocrat and a snob because he did not anticipate the arrival of the democracy of to-day or hail its possibility is about as judicial as it would be to characterize him as an oppressor because he did not foresee that the adventures of Raleigh were the first steps to a new England destined to revolt against the Mother Country, or as a Little Englander because he had no conception of a world-wide British Empire.

A Liberal Conservative

IT was Professor Dowden's view that Shakespeare would never fire a reader's mind with a political mission : certainly he laboured under no ultra revolutionary zeal as many another well-known poet has done. There seems to me little difficulty in deciding what Shakespeare should be labelled. If he had lived to-day he would have been a Conservative of the best type. In other words, his works make for what may be called Liberal-Conservatism : he would not have opposed a blank negative to all demands for reform : neither would he have mistaken the demagogue for a demi-god whose demands must be satisfied without question. Politicians of all shades of thought may go to Shakespeare and find texts for the faith that is in them.

He has been held by a Radical

to be Milton's inferior as a poet because Milton was republican whilst he was "a benighted monarchist." Concerning kings, Shakespeare was as a king of them all. He made kings his subjects, as the seventeenth century sonneteer put it, and he was an English king, as Carlyle asserted, whom no time or chance, no Parliament or combination of Parliaments, could dethrone. Kings had to do his behests as no Constitutional monarch has ever been called upon to do the behests of a people. How far Shakespeare was conscious of the sceptre he held can only be matter for conjecture. There is nothing in his method of approaching the great in State affairs to suggest that he was aware of his own peculiar might in the realms of Literature and Thought. On the contrary, it has been held, as we have seen, that Shakespeare was no better than a sycophant, and that he found virtues in the high-placed which he did not see in the lowly. Ruskin's later susceptibilities were wounded by the discovery that Shakespeare made his ideal woman, " his perfect shepherdess," Rosalind, a disguised princess. Ruskin said : " His miracle of the white island exultingly quits her spirit-guarded sands to be Queen of Naples, and his cottage Rosalind is extremely glad to get her face unbrowned again." It was a shock to Ruskin to find Shakespeare in the company of the conventional story-teller, as though the ideal of woman-hood were not in fact more likely to be embodied in one of gentle nurture than in a mere child of nature. Was Shakespeare as obsequious a creature as the superior person would have us believe ? The truth is, Shakespeare is for no class in particular. He is the poet of all—in the best sense of the word therefore the poet of democ-racy. He cannot legitimately be made to support the common people against the noble, the sovereign against his subject, as a mere matter of class prejudice or sycophantic truckling.

Every class may learn something from him : the King the necessity of good government ; the people that the kingly state is by no means a happy one ; the statesman that the views of the people at large cannot be lightly ignored, though popular verdicts may be unstable ; the agitator that order, loyalty and patriotism are essential to a country's prosperity and growth ; the sufferer that discontent is inevitable, and that in whatever sphere he is called on to act, it will be well to recollect that there are others, in their own way, combating troubles equally hard to endure. Was the man whose vision comprehended so much likely to be a partisan ? If the Socialist who has studied political economy till he has succeeded in confounding and confusing both his own and other people's sympathies, would go to

Shakespeare, he would see the government of a state reduced to its natural and simple proportions. The modern, like the ancient, Cassius declares in effect :

> I had as lief not be, as live to be
> In awe of such a thing as myself.

But the poet who penned that sentence penned many others showing the craving for equality to be chimerical as all Socialistic experimenters, if not Socialistic theorists, know it to be. Shakespeare goes to Nature for his chief witness. There is no obvious likeness between Canterbury in *Henry V* and Ulysses in *Troilus and Cressida;* the stories are as unlike as Agincourt and Troy ; the people are as widely separated as Greece and England. Yet Ulysses and Canterbury point one moral, which, of course, is Shakespeare's own drawn from his contemplation of Nature animate and elemental. Can anyone who claims to

be a democrat, something that is very
different from a mere demagogue who
would invert the order of the universe
and with it the very pyramid of society,
put either speech in the category
of the snob and the sycophant?
Ulysses knows why Troy, after seven
years' siege, still stands ; the Grecian
host is divided against itself, and his
speech is the most tremendous of all
indictments of faction in which neither
democracy nor any other régime can
thrive :

The speciality of rule hath been neglected ;
And look how many Grecian tents do stand
Hollow upon this plain, so many hollow fact-
    ions.
When that the general is not like the hive
To whom the foragers shall all repair,
What honey is expected ? Degree being viz-
    arded,
Th' unworthiest shows as fairly in the mask.
The heavens themselves, the planets and this
    centre
Observe degree, priority and place,
Insisture, course, proportion, season, form,
Office, and custom, in all line of order ;
And therefore is the glorious planet Sol
In noble eminence enthron'd and spher'd

SHAKESPEARE AND DEMOCRACY

Amidst the other ; whose med'cinable eye
Corrects the ill aspects of planets evil,
And posts, like the commandment of a King
Sans check, to good and bad. But when the
    planets
In evil mixture, to disorder wander,
What plagues and what portents ! what
    mutiny !
What raging of the sea, shaking of earth,
Commotion in the winds, frights, changes,
    horrors,
Divert and crack, rend and deracinate
The unity and married calm of States
Quite from their fixture ! O, when degree is
    shak'd
Which is the ladder to all high designs,
The enterprise is sick ! How could communities,
Degrees in schools, and brotherhoods in cities,
Peaceful commerce from dividable shores,
The primogenity and due of birth
Prerogative of age, crowns, sceptres, laurels,
But by degree, stand in authentic place ?
Take but degree away, untune that string,
And, hark, what discord follows ! Each string
    meets
In mere oppugnancy : The bounded waters
Should lift their bosoms higher than the shores
And make a sop of all this solid globe ;
Strength should be lord of imbecility,
And the rude son should strike his father dead :
Force should be right, or rather right and
    wrong,
(Between whose endless jar justice resides)
Should lose their names and so should justice
    too.

Then everything includes itself in power,
Power into will, will into appetite ;
And appetite, an universal wolf,
So doubly seconded with will and power,
Must perforce make an universal prey
And last eat up himself. Great Agamemnon,
This chaos, when degree is suffocate
Follows the choking.
And this neglection of degree it is,
That by a pace goes backward, with a purpose
It hath to climb. The general's disdained
By him one step below ; he, by the next ;
The next, by him beneath : so every step,
Exampled by the first pace of him that is sick
Of his superior, grows to an envious fever
Of pale and bloodless emulation ;
And 'tis this fever that keeps Troy on foot,
Not her own sinews. To end a tale of length,
Troy in our weakness stands, not in her strength.

Democracy will endure just so long as it recognizes the essential truths which Shakespeare puts into the mouth of Ulysses. When it degenerates into faction, chaos will ensue. Tyranny finds no support in Shakespeare, and his respect for degree is not respect for privilege but for order. The complement and commentary on Ulysses' speech is Canterbury's response to Exeter's suggestion that " Government,

though high and low and lower,
put into parts doth keep in one consent ; congruing in a full and natural
close, like music."

True ; therefore doth heaven divide
The state of man in divers functions,
Setting endeavour in continual motion ;
To which is fixed as an aim or butt,
Obedience ; for so work the honey bees ;
Creatures, that by a rule in nature teach
The act of order to a peopled kingdom.
They have a king and officers of sorts ;
Where some, like magistrates, correct at home,
Others, like merchants, venture trade abroad,
Others, like soldiers, armed in their stings,
Make boot upon the summer's velvet buds ;
Which pillage they with merry march bring
    home
To the tent royal of their Emperor ;
Who, busied in his majesty, surveys
The singing masons building roofs of gold ;
The civil citizens kneading up the honey ;
The poor mechanic porters crowding in
Their heavy burdens at his narrow gate ;
The sad ey'd justice, with his surly hum,
Delivering o'er to executors pale
The lazy yawning drove. I this infer—
That many things, having full reference
To one consent, may work contrariously—
As many arrows, loosed several ways,
Fly to one mark.

Rights and Power of the People

THE fact that Shakespeare never disguised from himself for one moment the necessity of grades in societies did not blind him to the rights of every section of the community. No man has made more complete recognition of the power of the people and the danger of grinding their faces by iniquitous laws. He knew that to deny them justice was to risk revolution, and whenever opportunity arose he emphasised a truth borne out by history, but ignored by Governments from time to time at the cost of national cataclysm. The lesson of the Revolution which brought many a noble head to the guillotine a century and three-quarters after Shakespeare's death, and made every Government in Europe look to its position and consider what it were wise and just to do to avert a disaster similar to that which overtook the French monarchy—that lesson was not Shakespeare's to learn. His plays teem with references which argue knowledge of a truth that many so-called statesmen have ignored until time for peaceful remedy had gone by. In *Henry IV* we find Westmoreland condemning the Archbishop of York for espousing the cause of " base and bloody " insurrection, and the Archbishop replies :

I have in equal balance justly weighed
What wrongs our arms may do, what wrongs
    we suffer
And find our griefs heavier than our offences.
We see which way the stream of time doth run
And are enforced from our most quiet sphere
By the rough torrent of occasion ;
And have the summary of all our griefs
When time shall serve, to show in articles
Which long ere this we offered to the King
And might by no suit gain an audience.
When we are wronged and would unfold our griefs
We are denied access unto his person
Even by those men that most have done us
    wrong.

To this very purport speaks the first citizen in *Coriolanus*. Menenius

Agrippa asks them why they assemble in the street with bats and clubs. And the answer is : " Our business is not unknown to the Senate, they have had inkling this fortnight what we intend to do, which we will now show them in deeds," and a little later he thus indicates their grievances in response to a suggestion that " the helms of the state " are their very good friends and care for their wants exceedingly. " Care for us ! True, indeed ! they never cared for us yet. Suffer us to famish and their store-houses crammed with grain : make edicts for usury to support usurers ; repeal daily any wholesome act established against the rich ; and provide more piercing statutes daily to chain up and restrain the poor. If wars eat us not up they will, and *there's* all the love they bear us."

Why, indeed, were the poor up in arms ? Not because they were irreconcilables and visionaries, but because their stomachs were empty and their rulers heeded not their woes. What authority surfeited on, they frankly declared would bring them relief, and they acted " in hunger for bread, not in thirst for revenge." The crisis here was the same that threatened in Henry VIII's time when overtaxation left men little margin even for the barest necessaries. Danger, we are told, served among them, and curses lived where prayers were wont to be. Shakespeare makes Henry VIII quick to perceive to what the trouble thus caused might lead, if not summarily checked, and instantly commands that to every country where the agitation against the excessive contributions levied on the people exists shall be despatched free pardons to all who have taken part in it.

There is nothing in all this to support the " anti-democratic bias " theory. When the commons were unfriendly, even in packed-parliament days, kings and statesmen had occasion to beware. Cardinal Wolsey paid a tribute to their powers by his anxiety to take credit for the remission of taxes which he had actually been instrumental in creating. He wished to stand well with the people. Coriolanus, again, who fought so hard against the popular will, who regarded the people with a bitterness of hatred probably unexampled, who never uttered a word of flattery to secure their suffrages and who ate what we should regard as the sour grapes of electioneering with an ill grace which he could not disguise, Coriolanus of all men had to seek safety from their anger, whilst his friend appealed to their leaders on his behalf. Richard II feared Bolingbroke because he had observed how his banished cousin had courted the common people, and later when Richard was deposed, Northumberland became fearful that the Commons would not be satisfied unless Richard subscribed to the document detailing the wrongs on account of which he had been deprived of his crown. In *Henry VI* Margaret shows that she dreads the effect of the flattery by which Humphrey has won the people's hearts, and after the unhappy Regent has been done to death, we get a picture of the Commons clamouring for the blood of his murderer. In *Richard III* Gloster is desirous of becoming the favoured of the people. He pretends to be very devout and with a Bible in his hand and a bishop on either side of him, refuses the sovereignty proffered by his friends. Buckingham's address, extolling virtues the murderer never had, and assuming that the shout of the few is the declaration of the many, is worthy of the most pretentious and self-deceiving of modern demagogues.

Shakespeare, we are pretty safe in saying, would have been a constitutionalist to the very finger-tips—as excellent an ornament of King George V's reign as he was of the time of good Queen Bess. He would never have sought unreasonably to oppose the nation's will. The last place where we might expect to find evidence of his readiness to admit the supremacy of the people perhaps is *Hamlet*. Laertes tells Ophelia not to think too much of the prince's avowal of love. Why? Because Hamlet

> May not as unvalued persons do
> Carve for himself; for on his choice depends
> The safety and health of the whole state
> And therefore must his choice be circum-
>   scribed
> Unto the voice and yielding of that body
> Whereof he is the head.

Coriolanus and Julius Cæsar

SHAKESPEARE is not indeed prepared to suggest that the people are always in the right. He leaves a fatalist impression, and says in effect : Do not resist that which is certain to prove stronger than yourself—very much the sort of thing that the late Lord Salisbury said to the House of Lords when he realised that the nation was united against the peers. Yet nowhere can we get a more vivid and inerradicable idea of the pendulum nature of the popular will than in Shakespeare. What is voted for one minute may be voted against the next. Shakespeare makes Coriolanus, who never tired of sounding the gamut of plebeian shortcomings, put the shiftiness of the Commons' heart in the extremest and most acrid form :

He that depends
Upon your favours swims with fins of lead

And hews down oaks with rushes. Hang ye !
   trust ye !
With every minute do you change a mind
And call him noble that was now your hate,
Him vile that was now your garland !

Mr. Harold Hodge, in a study of *Coriolanus*, said that he did not feel he knew any more about Shakespeare's own political leanings after reading the play than he did before. " Shakespeare had great insight into politics. That is obvious enough. He had thought about them ; he had opinions; but the artist was stronger than the politician," and as artist Shakespeare in *Coriolanus* does not, Mr. Hodge points out, give us either a high view of political life, or a type of true aristocracy. But if we read *Coriolanus* and qualify the political reflections it engenders by what we find elsewhere in Shakespeare, we have then surely the clue to the political philosophy of the dramatist. Thus judged we understand that Shakespeare himself would not have gone so far as *Coriolanus*, though we find in his works any number of instances of the instability of popular feeling. The Archbishop of York speaks of the " habitation giddy and unsure " of those who build on " the vulgar heart." Bagot refers to the " wavering Commons," and the Chorus which opens the second part of *Henry IV* talks of " the blunt monster with uncounted heads, the still discordant wavering multitude."

Just as Shakespeare saw the unwisdom of indifference to public grievances, so he understood the irresistible power for good or evil of the orator who has the popular ear. In *Coriolanus* at the bidding of the tribunes the people declare against Coriolanus within a few minutes of having promised to support him. In *Henry IV* Jack Cade, Buckingham and Clifford make the people, in response to their appeals, cry with the most irrational changefulness " God Save the King," " We'll follow Jack Cade," and " We'll follow the King and Clifford." Jack Cade is moved to exclaim " Was ever feather so lightly blown to and fro, as this multitude ! " When the keepers in the wood recognise the fugitive Henry VI, and decide to give him up to the Usurper, Henry takes a feather and says with no little force and justification :

Look, as I blow this feather from my face
And as the air blows it to me again,
Obeying with my wind when I blow
And yielding to another when it blows,
Commanded always by the greatest gust—
Such is the lightness of you common men.

The most remarkable instance is, of course, afforded by the events which followed the murder of Julius Cæsar. Brutus claimed to have taken part in that cowardly act out of pity to the general wrongs of Rome, and to have been moved by highest patriotic motives—motives which induce a man to forget himself, his friends, everything. He excused himself on

the ground that Cæsar aimed at being
crowned King, and we are always
reminded that Brutus obeyed the
unuttered command of Rome in the
step he took. When Cæsar was offered
the Crown, it is said the people applauded faintly ; when he refused it
they cheered as lustily as they knew
how. If Shakespeare conveys any
moral at all, he justifies one in saying
that had Cæsar accepted the Crown,
the people who cheered its refusal
would have applauded its acceptance.
The assassination of Cæsar was little
better than wanton butchery, and it
might have been thought that when
Shakespeare made Brutus explain his
motives to the mob, he would have
given the mob credit for sufficient
good feeling and good sense not to
cheer. But it seems almost as though
Shakespeare could not miss the chance
of affording signal illustration of the
manner in which the popular pendulum may be made to swing. Brutus

44

has hardly finished his speech, when Antony mounts the rostrum.

How little does Brutus realise the danger of leaving the man with ready tongue to deal with the facts, and how cleverly Antony insinuates what he hardly dare openly say at the moment ! He refers again and again to Brutus and Cassius as honourable men but with every reference heightens the complexion he puts on Cæsar's devotion to Rome. He must not tell the people how Cæsar loved them ; he must not read them Cæsar's will, because forsooth they are not stones but men. He moves them to tears ; then to fury ; and he keeps them well in hand, so that he may rub salt into the wounds as he inflicts them. And all the while he is perfectly conscious of the mischief he is doing. He obliterates utterly the memory of what Brutus has said. The popular cry is for vengeance, and Antony's oration has its issue in the suicide of Cassius and

Brutus. His own fate and that of Rome after he has attained power are, it is to be feared, not altogether peculiar. He had great eloquence, and there his gifts ended. Its mere possession induced his fellows to believe that he was a man of character and ability. " Words and weakness " was Gardiner's description of Cranmer, and it may hold good of many besides, including Mark Antony.

The Kingly State

SHAKESPEARE had a very exalted idea of the kingly state. He was impressed by the claims which the position of monarch makes on one who is still mortal and human. Few who take their conception of kingship from Shakespeare would, unless they had appetites for difficulty, wish to change places with the most fortunate monarch alive. It is the tragic side of the kingly state which Shakespeare emphasises. There are in his historical plays few of the lighter scenes of Court life, few touches of gaiety, and, if we except the Falstaffian element, little irresponsibility. Treason, and intrigue, and war's alarms are the notes on which he mainly rings the changes. From the manner in which he insists on the troubles that wait on kingship, it is fair to conclude that our prince of poets regarded the life of a Sovereign as wanting in those attributes which tend to make the existence of the ordinary citizen tolerable. Shakespeare was not dazzled by the fierce light which beats upon the throne. It rather, indeed, served to give him a better insight into the real conditions of a monarch's existence. Shakespeare managed to get behind the scenes in a way denied to ordinary mortals, and he saw the man's heart under the most gorgeous of regal trappings.

Whether it was that of a Richard II believing—like any Stuart—in his Divine appointment, of a Henry IV remembering the past, of a Henry V winning the love of his people and the respect of his enemies, or of a Henry VI with his semi-religious, peace-at-any-price leanings, Shakespeare perceived little in the kingly state to call for enthusiasm or envy. " How soon mightiness turns to misery " could almost be taken as a motto not merely for *Henry VIII*, but for all Shakespeare's historical plays. Richard's ruminations when his Kingdom has slipped from his grasp into the stronger hands of a Bolingbroke are but an exaggerated presentment of the Shakespearian view :

For God's sake let's sit upon the ground,
And tell sad stories of the death of kings,
How some have been depos'd, some slain in war,
Some haunted by the ghosts they have depos'd ;
Some poisoned by their wives, some sleeping
    kill'd ;
All murder'd—for within the hollow crown
That rounds the mortal temples of a king,
Keeps death his Court, and there the antic sits,
Scoffing his state and grinning at his pomp,
Allowing him a breath, a little scene,
To monarchise, be feared and kill with looks ;
Infusing him with self and vain conceit,
As if this flesh which walls about our life
Were brass impregnable : and humoured thus,
Comes at the last, and with a little pin
Bores through his castle wall, and—farewell king!

Well may Brackenbury, taking the Shakesperian view of things, exclaim that " Princes have but their titles for their glories." Why is it that the ship-boy, rocked " in the cradle of the rude

49

imperious surge," can close his eyes
in forgetfulness, when the king, in
" the calmest and most stillest night,"
lies wide awake ? " Uneasy lies the
head that wears a crown " is Shakespeare's, as well as Henry IV's answer.
Even Prince Hal recognises this, and
when reproved by his dying father for
trying on the golden circlet ere the
breath is out of the King's body, the
son makes ready response. 'Twas not
vainglory, but a desire to try con-
clusions with an enemy that had
murdered his father. He upraids this
" best of gold " as " the worst of gold "
for the cares it brought his sire. In the
years to come, when Henry V is adding
glory on glory to his name in France,
he asks himself what kings have that
others have not, save ceremony ? And
what is ceremony ? Will it give kings
the heart's ease other men enjoy ?
Will it give the health of the beggar's
knee which it commands ? How little
the peasant who sleeps soundly o'

nights, year in, year out knows of the
anxious hours spent by the conscien-
tious ruler who preserves the peace,
upholds the honour, and maintains
the welfare of his country for the
benefit of his people. Not extraordinary
was it that if this was Shakespeare's
idea of the kingly state when a Henry
IV or V was concerned, he should
make a weakling like Henry VI long
to be a subject more than subject ever
longed to be a king. It was a special
characteristic of the nineteenth century
—a characteristic which eighteen
months ago had reached a dangerous
fullness of development—to exploit
grievances, and it was the great
achievement of demagogy to show
the classes and the masses that their
interests were separate and distinct.
Shakespeare would repay careful
study if he did no more than make it
clear that " we are not all alone unhappy," but that " this wide and
universal theatre presents more woeful

pageants than the scenes we play in."
Does not Richard II put a host of
political experience in briefest space
when he says that in his person he
plays the parts of many people, " and
none contented ? "

" Sometimes am I king.
Then treason makes me wish myself a beggar,
And so I am ; then crushing penury
Persuades me I was better when a king."

When Shakespeare's Kings failed
in their high office he adjudged their
failure by the gauge of humanity in
general ; when they succeeded he
gave them credit due to achievement
in exceptional conditions. He concerned himself with abstract questions
neither of Divine Right nor Diabolic
Wrong, as Carlyle would have said,
but with the doings of men who were
none the less men because they were
placed high above their fellows in the
ordering of society.

Even-handed Justice

SHAKESPEARE'S political and social philosophy is perhaps summed up in the words of the Bastard in *King John*, who says :

> Whiles I am a beggar, I will rail,
> And say there is no sin but to be rich
> And being rich my virtue then shall be
> To say there is no vice but beggary.

The more fully we share this view, the more heartily we shall commend the impartiality with which Shakespeare handles the facts of life and history. In surest proof of this impartiality there is the object lesson in equality before the law supplied by Henry V. When the King bids Exeter release the man who, in his cups, railed against the royal person, Cambridge, Grey and Scroop urge him to award the fellow some punishment, however much the sovereign's heart may prompt him to mercy. Henry refers gratefully to their care for his person and then hands them papers which show that he is cognisant of their own treachery.

They crave mercy and Henry answers :

The mercy which was quick in us but late
By your own counsel is suppressed and kill'd.
You must not dare for shame to talk of mercy :
For your own reasons turn into your bosoms,
As dogs upon their masters, worrying them !

These words, if written by a playwright to-day, would be regarded as a plum for the gallery. They argue a love of even-handed justice calculated to win the applause of the patron of a Lyceum melodrama. Let the passage bear witness that in an age when the poor had few rights, Shakespeare held the balance steady and placed high and low on a footing of equality before the blindfolded goddess. The quality of justice was as little strained in him as the quality of mercy.

The Kingdom of Poetry

DEMOCRACY to succeed must have leaders; the man on top is as indispensable to democracy as to tyranny; Shakespeare was the poet of leadership, and false leaders, enemies of the Commonwealth, whether a Jack Cade or a Coriolanus, he never allowed to stand forth as a hero. To deny Shakespeare's interest in, and sympathy with, the common people is to rob his patriotism, which no one has called in question, of much of its fire and meaning. As he gloried in England and her achievements down to the opening years of the seventeenth century, so we may be sure he would have gloried in the achievements of a Britain which has planted both Empire and Democracy in the lands beyond the seas which were only being explored in his day. From the loins of his England have sprung the great democracies of the United States of America, Canada, Australia, and New Zealand. The daring and the strong right arm of the adventurers who were then going forth into Eastern Seas in search of markets have given the England he knew the Empire of the Indies. For the upbuilding of the Empire, for the enlightened despotism by which it is ruled ; for the freedom which has been found the surest guarantee of the loyalty of peoples of every shade of political thought and every religion, for the ideals which move us to seek a union of which no empire ancient or modern provides a pattern, may we not give some measure of credit to Shakespeare ? Mr. F. R. Benson has finely expressed the thought which links up the Democratic Imperial sentiment of to-day with the author of *King Henry V* :

"Has History ever recorded an Empire whose component parts have little, if any, formal bond, whose units are not obliged to send one soldier or to spend one shilling, and yet are giving to the uttermost their heart's treasure and their blood—for what ? For the song-word of our race, for Freedom. Who but a poet can realise such an ideal so simple, so complex, so individual, so universal, so free, yet so self-governed learning from the needs of all men, taking colour and shape from all races. From the four quarters of the earth they come, and with them the elder Aryan from India, often misunderstood, often misjudged, in the moment of national danger he offers his aid ' all I possess.' And so the practical poets with the will to the good not merely the will to power have wended their way to the West by road and river and stormy sea, singing as they went for joyousness of their strong, full life. The melody of their march is the music of great deeds, the blending of many bloods, the reconciling of many antagonisms round a common ideal of noble citizenship : a common ideal of Empire, not for conquest, or exploitation, or lust of greed, but an Empire for expansion and association ; an Empire, which in terms of patriotism and intensification of national life shall bring the world a step nearer to the Brotherhood of Man. Of such is the kingdom of Poetry, and Shakespeare wears its crown."

Shakespeare stood and stands for Democracy, for Empire, for Humanity ; his message for all mankind and for all time is Nature's own ; it will ring down the ages, a challenge to prejudice, a clarion call to Patriotism.

Foolscap 8vo.   2s. Net

SECOND IMPRESSION READY

ROYAL AUCTION BRIDGE AND NULLOS

With Illustrative Hands and Problems

By

TAUNTON WILLIAMS

Mr. Taunton Williams is a guide, philosopher and friend in the practical application of the most up-to-date rules, and gives illustrative hands which will show the average player how to make the most of his cards.

" There is something unusually fascinating in the manner in which the author deals with his theme. He has human as well as expert knowledge at his command."—*Daily Graphic.*

"A very thorough compendium of the game and its intricacies."—*Sheffield Daily Telegraph.*

McBRIDE, NAST & CO., LTD.